Book of Poems 4

Addiction

My heart starts pounding.
The sweat starts dripping down my face.
Soaked to the point of being cold,
I am loud and proud.

When people say that I have done well,
I am loud and proud.
I tend to be smug.
I like it when I am right.
I hate it when I am wrong.

When I help someone,
I feel as if I am soaring.
When I please someone,
I feel as if my wings have grown.

When I displease someone,
It unnerves me.
I do not like it one bit.
I want to whine and cry about it.

When I see the number on the scale,
When my clothes fit just a little bit more loosely than yesterday,
I am loud and proud.
I like to brag.
I like to say, “Oh, look what I did!”
I feel so big and so important.
Something so tiny turns into something so big.

When I make the slice,
Deeper and deeper,
Longer and longer,
I am standing on the roof of the tallest building.
Knowing it is wrong,
I still do it.

When something comes up,
Someone else falls,
I like to jump in.
I like to pick up where that person left off.

I like to avoid the trouble I tend to cause.
Maybe it is a part of me.
Maybe I am sneaky like that.
You will never know.

I thrive on this kind of thing.
It truly is sickening.
There is nothing I can do.
I can stop it, but there is no point.
I do not want to stop it.
I am too afraid to stop it.
What will be left of me without trouble?

This is one addiction I cannot comprehend.
This is one addiction that leaves me clueless.
I am in shock.
I cannot believe I am genuinely like this.

Be aware of this mean spirit of mine.
It strikes when we all least expect it.
I can lie.
I do not like the truth.
A lie is more interesting than the truth.

I am loud and proud about this.
I simply do not care.
Everything is shoved aside.
This is my addiction.
This is my thing I have going for me.

I take the pill and drink the wine.
I have myself trapped.
These chains refuse to unhand me.
My soul is rotting away within my flesh.

I am truly a hateful human being.
Maybe I no longer have that privilege,
The privilege to be called a human being.
I no longer feel like one.
I am the failed, scorned, artistic woman.
There is nothing like those kinds.

Do not reach your hand out to me.
I do not need saving.
I am sick.
I am truly sick.
My head is not screwed on properly.
I should care about things.
I know I should.

Alone With My Thoughts

First point to be made perfectly clear,
I am not suicidal.
Okay?

Now that we got that straight,
I was wondering if anyone would care if I were to die.

Would anyone look over their shoulder to the sky?
Would anyone remember me?
Who would?
Why?
I am just thinking is all.

I am learning to love myself more.
These days,
It is difficult to love my mom body.
I am getting frustrated with my child too.
That does not mean I give up.

If you look into the clouds,
Would you see my face?
What would you do?
How would that make you feel?

I do not have many friends.
Most of the women I know tend to goof off in life.
There is nothing wrong with a little fun.
I am not saying I am against it.
What I am against is,

Getting so drunk that you fall into a wall.
If you get drunk,
Do not break the windows.

People make fools of themselves.
I am not making a fool of myself here.
Am I?
I do not know what you have against me.

What do I have against you?
Nothing at all.
I just am who I am.
Please, do not try and change who I am.

I am sick of society.
Everyone wants to be that skinny girl.
Everyone wants to be fly.
Make up and clothes do not cover up your bad attitude.

Who am I to judge?
Right?
Am I judging?
I do not mean to judge.
I do not get along with shallow people.
People who think they get a free pass,

Erase yourself from my sight.

I cannot stop thinking about these things.
This is a talk poem.
This expresses me.
No one is involved in making this poem.

Who is my audience?
Probably no one.
Will I still publish this poem?
Yes, even though it sounds horrible in my mind.

My brain is always full of mindless chatter.
I have to get it out somehow.
I will go mad if I do not.
You do not want a female Mad Hatter in your wake.
Trust me.
That is not a good thing.

I have not typed a poem in a while.
I have a hard time coming up with words.
Yeah, that expresses this poem that probably makes no sense.
It is up to the reader to try and decipher my words.
It is not my fault I feel misunderstood.
Believe me.

The public thinks I am annoying.

I may seem like I know it all.
Someone in my class one day at least thought I was one.
Yes, I do know what it feels like to be suicidal.
No, I did not know what happened with the person who killed himself.
I only heard rumors that may or may not have been true.

So, some of you think I am clueless.
I do not need to care about this aspect.
I only know as much as I know.
In high school,
I was not treated well at all.

These days,
People think it is a miracle that I have a kid.
Was I really that bad?
Some of you do not know how to address someone like me.
Get out of my face.
Come back when you can be kinder.

Alone

I hate being alone.
Being along is too tempting.

I’m always alone.
I’m a lonely person.

My thoughts race.
My own anxieties make me feel so out of place.
I don’t belong in this world.
I might belong in the next world.
I don’t know.

My thoughts are so irritating.
I can’t stand them.
It’s so difficult to stand up to them.
I feel as if I’m losing my mind.

I talk all the time.
It helps to make the noise in my head a little less.
This world of self-hate is one I try to ignore.
The world outside of me isn’t so kind.
This adds fuel to the fire.

Sometimes I like being alone.
I can dwell within these hopeless thoughts.
I can make myself empty.
I hate being alone because I hate liking that I feel this way.
The darkness inside of me is often reigned in.

This empty feeling deep inside of me,
This empty void,
Where nothing grows,
Not even the flowers,
I don't know what to do with it.
Should I put it high on a shelf?

I hate that I like feeling this way.
It's madness.
It makes no sense.
Why do I like feeling this way?
It's to my enjoyment.
It's to my entertainment.

Maybe I just want attention.
That right there adds to the puzzle.
I want to be loved.
I want a good man to love me.
Don't I have that?

I want to be greedy here for just a second.
I want to want more here for just a second.
It's a mystery to me.
My words all run together.

I hate that I like the way I feel.

This isn't supposed to be.
This isn't supposed to exist.
This empty feeling is something I like.
I'm not supposed to like it so much.
Maybe I'm all messed up in the head.

I'll die.
I'll kill myself off.
If that's what I want,
If that's my desire,
I will do it.

I will lie.
I will make things up.
I will plaster a smile on my face.
I will hide the dark truth of my nature.
No one will know.
No one will understand anyway.

I feel empty inside and I like it.
I want to remain here.
I want to drown.
I want to jump.

I want to hurt.

I want to burn.

Return me to ash.

Return me to the dirt where I belong.

I'm waiting for my death.

I want to run towards it.

I yearn it with all of my being.

Pull me into the darkness of despair.

I want to remain hopeless.

This is why I hate being alone.

These thoughts are so tempting.

I know why I'm here.

I know why I want to leave.

Shroud me in eternal darkness.

This is where I belong.

Please, don't reach a hand out to save me.

I don't want to be saved.

Always Searching for Words

Staring up at the clouds on a halfway cloudy day,

I wonder what everything means.

Should I wander astray?

Should I wake up and taste the greens?

For once in my life,
I want words.
For once in my strife,
I want more than just odd verbs.

It doesn't matter how,
I want more words to describe everything.
It doesn't matter now.
I want the wonders those words will bring.

I've got an itch to scratch.
There are no words to describe this emotion.
This cheesy poem is quite the catch.
There are no words to describe the commotion.

AUGH!!!! It's time to go out of pattern here!
I don't care!
I'm out of words.
Leave it be.
Like I've already told you,
I'm always on a search.
This search sometimes comes up empty.

It’s like my voice is being heard.
These words are what I would say.
Read every single line.
This is me.
This is who I am.

Curious as can be,
Ah, let me see…
Um…I’m always searching for words?
Ha! That’s right!

This poem is in a different style.
I’m sure of it!
Go on and make fun of it.
I dare you.
Maybe you will fall face first into a puddle.

Actually, that was kind of evil of me.
Sorry!
Maybe not sorry?
Am I breaking the fourth wall again?
I think I am.

Oh boy!
Stop! Stop it now!

This is so not humorous.
This will not amuse anyone.

Like I've said,
I'm always searching for words.
I'm just way too curious!

Anger So Numb

I wish that I could just feel something.
Anything but anger will do.
I've grown numb to my surroundings.
The only exception is anger.

I don't know why this is happening.
I wish I could just fix it and move on.
My heart continues to grow colder.
These words are being read from the outside.
They aren't sinking into my soul.

I wish that I could just feel something more than anger.
All I feel is this relentless anger.
I can't release it.
It isn't enough to just release a little bit of it.
I try and try to hold it all in.

The dam will very soon overflow.
There will very soon be an uncontrollable flood.
I want to feel something more than just anger.
I'm numb to everyone and everything besides anger.

I'm always glowing red.
I'm always feeling hot.
My mouth never takes a holiday.
I'm always working up a sweat.
My words are always tumbling around each other.

Part of me is content to remain this way.
The other part of me wants more than this.
I find this really weird.
The anger always flows freely inside of me.
It's always building up.

My anger is ready to burst out into the world around me.
You'd better watch out.
It's a struggle to control it.
I want to feel something more than this numbing anger.

I bring myself down when I want to hit something.
I always want to slice myself up to bits.

I hate myself.
I hate what I've become.
I'm so much more cold hearted than before.

I used to be more rays of sunshine.
I used to believe more.
Now all I've got is this numbing anger.

I get upset when someone critiques me.
Why must I make such a fool out of myself.
"From now on" and "I will" or "I won't" is all I have to say.
These words are just dumb.

I can't get out of this hole I'm in.
I can't get away from the claws of this numbing anger.
It's always there.
It doesn't matter where I go or who I'm with.

I know that there is more to life than this.
The realization is there.
I just don't want to face it at times.
All I want to do is claw at myself.

I want to tear myself apart.
Don't try and cure me of this disease.

You always think you know it all.
You don't know a thing about me.

There has to be more to life than this numbing anger.
I'm falling deeper into this grave I've dug for myself.
The battle inside never ceases.
I can't always say my angered words.
I can't always put a finger on things.
I'm numb to everything except anger.

Anxiety

Sometimes my anxiety is so high.
It gets to the point where I don't care who I hurt.
I'll try to get what I want.
I'm an evil little monster.

All my emotions rise up from deep within.
I just don't care anymore.
I'm so tired of caring.
Don't you ever get tired of caring?

I want to yank all my hair out.
I want to punch myself in my own heart.

I need to cause my own pain.
I don't know what to do with myself anymore.

I'm visibly triggered.
Isn't it obvious?
Whom shall I hurt?
Oh, I'm sorry.
Wait, no I'm not.
I've hurt you.
Now go away.

Please, just leave me alone.
I'm just a lonely girl.
My heart reeks of defeat.
It's all right.
It doesn't matter anymore.
I can take care of myself.

I'll lay everything down.
I'll go out with style.
Burn me up with your lies.
Shoot me down with your words.
I'll take it just like I take everything else.

I'm a hard worker.

I’m kind.
Sometimes I just don’t care.
I’m not always in my right state of mind.

My anxiety runs high.
I’m hated by life itself.
It’s my fate to suffer so.
I’ll run and run far away.
This state of mind will always catch up with me.

I’m not going anywhere.
I’ll continue to drift amongst everything.
It all floats around me.
I can handle this for just a little while longer.
It doesn’t matter if I think I can’t.
I’m knocking on that window.
I’m watching from the outside.
I want to be let in.

I’m unsure about myself most of the time.
Can’t you tell with my hesitation?
Can’t you tell with my stumbling feet?
Sometimes I just don’t care.
Sometimes I just want to break free.

Can I close my eyes now?
Can I not worry about anyone or anything now?
I don't want you.
I don't think I even want me.

Things can go on like this for a while, can't they?
I don't know.
All I thought I knew,
All I thought that confirmed me,
It's all gone with the wind.

I float amongst the uncertainty.
I live this life of mine.
I'll never be at peace.
It doesn't matter to me how long I live.
Can I close my eyes?
Can I not worry?
I can't, can I?

All the times I wrap my hands around my neck,
All the times I try to choke out my worries,
I can't, can I?
I'm a coward.
I can be mean, disrespectful and argumentative.
Sometimes I just don't care.

It doesn’t always matter to me who I hurt.

I want to hurt myself.
I want to only hurt myself.
Maybe I will when the end comes.
I’m clinging for now.
I’ve always been clingy.
Why not to life as well?
Why not self-destruction?

Please, won’t you come get me?
I’m just this unknown chick.
I’m lost in a world full of vultures.
Everyone wants something.
Everyone just has to feed upon my worst fears.
Ruthless vultures.
Cruel and heartless.

Beautifully Broken Nonsense

I am broken.
You win my heart as if it is a token.
I am beautifully broken.
I don’t know what you were hopin’.

How have I gotten into this place?
I can't breathe in this small space.
I let things fall around me.
I sit back and watch as I drink my tea.

Life can be sweet.
I see you there and our eyes meet.
Life can be tart.
Did I just cause you to have a brain fart?

Good, I have confused more than just myself.
Ah, screw it!
This poem ain't goin' so well.
So sue me!
Don't judge me!

I'm the boss here.
It's my life.
You have no say in it.
I'm in control.

Ha!
Here I smile at you.
Just forget about letting things fall around me!
Like that would ever happen.

Or maybe it would?
Who knows?

This train of thought is goin' nowhere.
AUUUUGH, COME ON!
Okay, okay, it is time to think.
I sound like a mad woman.
Maybe I have gone insane.
Who knows?

I'm on the war path.
Don't get in my way.
I've decided what I want.
Now it's time to take out the trash.

I've given a voice to my words.
I don't care if they don't make sense.
That's your job.
You're my beloved reader.
Go and make sense of this poem!

I leave you with this.
I part ways with this message.
It comes from the bottle deep within my heart.
It's like a message in a bottle.

Quite the romantic tale, isn't it?

Say, what's the difference between romance and lust?
Some people have this wild sexual desire.
I don't like sexualizing anything.
I feel like it's unholy.
Maybe that's just me.

I'm as random as random can be.
What do you think the purpose of this poem is?
Sit up straight and listen to my words!
Stop clowning around and give me a straight answer!

I keep piling thing after thing.
My whole world reeks of overwhelming.
It's oozing out of the walls of my bedroom.
The message in the bottle is sealed.
It's airtight.
Other things have it vacuumed shut.

This poem is just a bunch of nonsense.
I can't keep myself in one place.
You already know this!
Why am I so bossy?
Well, my dear, that's because I am the boss.

Bells of Revolution

Look into her baby doll eyes.
She is not your enemy.
Baby, honey, sweetheart.

Dare you stand in her corner?
Endure the scrutiny.
Whisper into her ear when she is weeping.
Tell her everything will be okay.

Come on, come on!
Let us ring the bells of revolution!
It is time to start.
Stand up for the little lady in the corner.
Stand up for the tears she sheds.

Ring the bells of revolution!
Ring them loud and clear.
Let everyone hear them from a distance.
Stand up for what is true.

So what?
Go on and point the finger.
There are people just like her.

They are from a distant land.

Let the harsh memories out.
The sharp tongues cut deep.
Make her bleed out and see what you get.
Crush her heart into a million pieces and see what you get.

Come on, come on!
Let us ring the bells of revolution!
It is time to start.
Stand up for the little lady in the corner.
Stand up for the tears she sheds.

It is time to stand for what is right.
Baby doll, please, do not cry.
Everyone will already cry for you.
Just look into the eyes of the one who is innocent.

Reap what you sow.
There will be a day when things will come back at you.
Your fires will no longer rage.
Your sharp tongue will no longer cut into her.

Come on, come on!
Let us ring the bells of revolution!

It is time to start.
Stand up for the little lady in the corner.
Stand up for the tears she sheds.
Stand up, stand up.
It is time to stand up, stand up.

Stand for all that is fair.
Do not be fooled by what is unfair.
Do not be pulled into a world of darkness.
So what?
You are a living wreck.

Help us pick ourselves up once again.
Place one foot in front of the other.
Walk a straight line deep into your destiny.
Help her along.

Do not fear.
Let us not go along with the flow.
Come on, come on!
Let us ring the bells of revolution!
It is time to start.
Stand up for the little lady in the corner.
Stand up for the tears she sheds.

It is time to stand up, stand up!
It is the right thing to do.
The world is a cruel place.
Why must we make it worse?
Why must we add to it?
There is nothing to gain by the darkness.

Stand your ground.
There are heavy times ahead of us.
Right now, right now.
It is time to start thinking right now.
How can we help one another?
How can we spread hope?

Do not cheat yourself of this light.
It is better than sleeping deep into the darkness.
Baby doll, little lady, she is not your enemy.
She only wants your love.
She only wants what she feels she deserves.

Come on, come on!
Let us ring the bells of revolution!
It is time to start.
Stand up for the little lady in the corner.
Stand up for the tears she sheds.

Stand up, stand up for what is right and true!

Let us ring the bells!

Ring the bells of revolution.

Say your prayers.

Live your dreams.

Go through life like this.

Bo-Bo-Boing!

"I swear, lock me out and I'm going to kill you!"

"Hee hee! You're locked out!"

"Alright, that's it!"

GRRRRRAAAAAH, WHAT'S A GIRL GOTTA DO?!

Grab a ball and bo-bo-boing on your head!

Grab my heart and bo-bo-boing against yours.

Toss me around and get what's coming.

My mischievous smile comes easy.

You crack me up.

I'm half of you and you're half of me.

"You and your cheesy poems."

"Shut up and leave me alone!"

GRRRRAAAAAH, WHAT'S A GIRL GOTTA DO?!

Grab a ball and bo-bo-boing away!

Grab my hand and kiss, kiss, kiss away.
Hold me tightly in your arms.
Keep the fears and insecurities at bay.

"Am I pretty?"
"No. You're ugly."
"Shut up!"
AUUUUGH, YOU'RE SO ANNOYING!!!!!!!

Bo-Bo-Boing you make my heart go.
Bo-Bo-Boing like a bouncy ball.
Words that may seem hateful,
Words that may not seem normal,
Are made clear by your mischievous smile.

"Get off me! You're heavy!"
"Hey! Just what are you trying to say?!"
"You're fat! Now get off!"
AUUUUGH, YOU MAKE ME SO MAD!!!!!!!

In your own little weird way,
You make my heart go Bo-Bo-Boing.
Even if you did just lock me out of my own apartment.
GRRRRRR!!!!!!!!!!!!

Bo-Bo-Boing goes my heart!

Bo-Bo-Boing goes the ball on your head!

"Hey! Stop that!"

"Oh my? Have I made you mad?"

"Seriously! Will you quit?!"

Ha! I make you mad too!

While it may seem like we're always bickering,

We're really involved in a playful banter.

Teasing one another,

Until our laughter echoes off the walls.

Breaking Out

You cannot tame me.

You cannot control me.

That is my job and my job alone.

Only I can tame myself.

Only I can control myself.

What is perfect control?

What does it look like?

Well, it is kind of like busting out of a cage.

I feel myself emerging.

I may not be graceful, but at least I am breaking out.

This prison that you have put me in,
I have taken control as of right now.
I have made myself my own prison.
I am the gatekeeper.

Your eyes gleam with delight.
Why are you so proud?
I know you have your passionate hate.
I know where I stand with you.

Do not reach your hand out to me.
Do not touch me.
I will bite you.
I will pull out your hair.
I will scratch out your eyeballs.

Call me insane.
Call this a curse.
Honestly, I do not know myself.
I am living in my own Hell.
I have created it myself.

My thoughts chase their tails.
I have nothing but tall tales to tell.

My lips never stop moving.
I say and do before I think about it.

The choices I have made for myself,
Albeit good or bad,
I do want them to disappear into the past.
They belong in the past forever.

I am watching my life as if it were a movie.
The scenes are full of blood and gore.
My heart is in shambles.
It bleeds endlessly from the thorns that poke at it.

My emotions are all over the place.
Sometimes I do not feel a single thing.
Not a single tear can be shed.
I am all out.
I am a quickly fading image.

I am not who I thought I was.
I reject this person I have become.
I am annoying.
I even annoy myself at times.

I need to break out of this Hell.

I have put myself here.

I am the one to blame.

No one else is forcing me to remain here.

I need to break out.

Here I go.

I am breaking out.

I am releasing myself.

I am closing my eyes.

I am taking a deep breath.

Here I go.

It is time for me to take a step back.

It is time for me to allow God to control things.

I am not worried.

It is a struggle to remain not worried.

I refuse to worry even through the struggle.

My spirits are good.

I am high on my own self.

There is no drug better than life itself.

God created life.

I am a part of the life God has created.

I do not need anyone.

God is it.
He is the only one I need right now.
I refuse to fool around with others.
Please, understand.
Keep your hearts locked away from me.

I do not hold the key to open you up.
God does that.
Maybe one day I will grow with you.
Maybe.
One day.
There is hope.

Calls of Reality

Let it ring, let it ring.
Please, let's not answer.
I don't care.
Push out the reality that is me.

I'm living my own little world.
I don't care to see.
What damage does it make?

I'm currently not here.

Let's push ourselves away from one another.
I'm not answering that phone.

It gives me chills.
You're such a child.
I want to forget.
I don't want to play this game.

I'm a sappy romantic.
I'm also cold and hard.
What my eyes see is what my soul sees.
I can't see you anymore.

It's up to you to make sense of my words.
Your heart refused mine so long ago.
My heart still yearns for that warm touch.
You're so tough.

Why not pay me a visit?
Are you really that far gone?
I need you.
I want you.

I can't help this feeling.
Your hands caressing me,

That's what I want.
I want to be set ablaze.

Make my entire being melt away in your arms.
I need your electrifying touch.
I can see your fingers running along my moist skin.
You make me hot for you.

I can't breathe.
I close my eyes.
Your lips are like little feathers.
I can feel your warmth with my brain.

My thighs are leaking fluid from my pores.
My loins are aching for you.
Every part of me screams your name.
More, more, I want more.

I'm on fire just thinking about you.
I know who you are.
Have you forgotten me?
Your tongue on my breasts,
It's so satisfying.

I need that climax.

I need you inside me.
I need that release.
I want to be high on your love.
Why can't you remember what we had?

Please, come back to me.
Please, come back to my aching heart.
My entire being screams your name.
Have you forgotten with time gone by?

I can't make up my mind.
With what I picture in my mind,
With my urges,
Maybe it's not that I want you,
Maybe it's just the thought of that amazing touch.
Perhaps I want to experience that again.
I need to dive deeper into the red.

I can't answer the call of reality right now.
I'm currently under this spell.
I want more.
I need more.
Give me my treat.
Don't just dangle it in front of me.

Clear Head

I feel like I have a clear sense of mind.
There is nothing there.
I tend to space out.
I do not think about anyone or anything.

I know I am just here.
My body moves automatically.
I can see you there.
Why do you stare at me with such steely eyes?

I do not know who is more void of all emotion.
Is it you or is it me?
I am like a machine.
I do not feel anything.

I know what I am supposed to feel.
Sadness.
Anger.
I am supposed to cry out to God.
I am supposed to ask Him why.
I am supposed to ask Him what to do.

I am lost.

I want to live.
I need to survive.
I cannot sink deeper into this void.
I have lost all sense of who I am.

Sometimes I feel pure bliss.
That is just about it.
I am always smiling and dancing.
I always have a voice to sing.

Is it just me?
Am I imagining things?
I may or may not need to worry about this.
Maybe I am just professional.

I look at this music video with laughs.
Nothing can hurt me.
The sun always rises.
It does not matter if I get into trouble.

I can hear the world.
I cannot hear myself.
I need to not sink even more into this dark world.
Call me emo, but I know I am right.

I am a 90s kid.
The emo thing was there.
I grew up with it.
I do not care if it is out of style.
These times do not scare me.

I have been here all night.
I will remain here all day.
You cannot get rid of me.
I have a clear head.

Out of mind.
Out of sight.
I have a clear head.
My mind is cool like water.
It is a smooth flow.

I may be emotionless.
I am professional just by chance.
I do not allow myself to lose my head.
There is this other side to me.

Do not judge me.
Do not try and fix me.
I am who I am.

I am not perfect.
I am worth it.
I am beautiful.
I am not hurt by anything or anyone.
I refuse to be.

Confidence

Hello.
Goodbye.
Just like that,
It's here and then it's gone.
It's like a ghost ghosting by.

I'm fierce and then I'm not.
I'm annoying and then I'm not.
You're worried and then you're not.
Which one is it?
Make up my mind for myself.

Why does confidence fade?
Why do I always get choked up on my words?
I can't make a single sound.
I can't say no.
All I can say is yes.

Why am I such a people pleaser?
Why do I always care what others think?
Just because I'm out there,
Just because I'm loud,
You always have to question whether or not this is actually a thing.
Well, it is with me.

When I make mistakes,
When the outcome isn't what I wanted,
I scream and cry on the inside.
I cringe at how I behave.
I cringe at what I say.

Just this once,
From here on out,
I want things to change.
I want the confidence to change my circumstances.
I want to be me.

Please, don't stop me.
Please, don't tell me I'm being stupid.
Please, don't tell me it's too much.
My confidence can't remain lost.

I know what I want.
I know who I want to be.
This is me.
This is the real person living inside my heart.

I wasn't so sure at first.
I didn't want to scare people away.
I didn't want to scare myself away.
I have this version of myself that's confident.
I want to be that person.

Demons

"There is nothing wrong with you," says a voice deep inside.
"Yes, there is something wrong with me," she tells the voice deep inside.
"Well then, why didn't you say something?"
"I don't want to sound like I'm seeking attention."

Doctors are supposed to be professionals.
Nurses are supposed to be professionals.
No one has grasped what is wrong.
She's not saying anything.

"Do you not want to admit it," asks the voice.
She closes her eyes and shakes her head sadly.

"What is this? Is it thrilling? Does it turn you on?"

"Please, stop saying stuff like that," she tells the voice.

"I have all the power," claims the voice.

"No, you don't."

"You've just given me all the power."

"What makes you say that?"

"I want you to look like those models," says the voice in her head.

"I do too, but I hate being sleepy."

"You need to go workout even when you're sleepy."

"If I do that, will I be able to admit I have a problem?"

"Your problem isn't serious enough," taunts the voice.

"I think it's serious no matter how it looks," she replies.

"You can't talk, but I can."

"Do I eat or not," she wonders.

"What do you want to eat," asks the voice.

"I don't know," she answers.

"Tell me exactly what you want."

"I'm not good enough, am I?"

"You're not sick enough."

"When will anyone notice," she asks the voice.

"Never," taunts the voice.

"Right. Unless I'm so underweight that it's noticeable."

"That's right. Like when you were in high school," tempts the voice.

"I can't go back to the way I was," she tells the voice.

No matter how she tries to fight it,

She just can't win.

It sucks her right back in once more.

Her chest hurts.

Her heart pounds.

She's out of breath.

Sweat drenches her skin and her clothes cling to her.

"I still have this belly," she tells the voice.

"Get rid of it," says the voice.

"It's not that easy. It takes time and patience."

"You don't have time or patience."

"I can learn to have that."

"You know you can't," says the voice.

"What if I make myself sick," she asks the voice.

"That's a good idea," the voice tempts back.

"It's tempting, but I'd rather not."

"Who cares what you think?"

"I care."

"No. You just care about what other people think."

"True."

She fights back with every she's got.

Her emotions are all over the place.

She feels disconnected from the world.

It's her own inner demons she's battling against.

Sometimes her heart isn't in it.

Sometimes she gives in.

There are times when she overthrows her tempting ideals.

Maybe she's stressed.

Maybe she's depressed.

None of it sounds cool either way.

It is what it is.

Maybe she needs to get some help.

Maybe she just needs some encouragement from others.

"I hate you, you know that," she tells the voice.

"Well, the feeling is mutual," replies the voice.

"I want to shatter you."

"I want to destroy you from the inside out."

"You're making me have an eating disorder," she tells the voice.

"Honey, you don't have an eating disorder yet."

"It's getting there."

"You don't deserve to have an eating disorder."

Do Away With

Say, have you lost faith in me?
I have lost faith in you.
Do you know who I am anymore?
I do not know who you are anymore.
Maybe you were not who you made me believe you were.

You are hateful.
You are mean.
I think you have lost your mind.
I do not think you have any sanity left.
You may think the same of me.
I think it more true about you than it is about me.

When you feel all is lost,
When you feel yourself at the end of your rope…
Well, I just do not think you understand what I mean.
I know.
Why do you not just do away with yourself.

You are ungrateful.
You take everything for granted.
It was you who I wanted.
I wanted your arms around me.
I wanted your lips on mine.

I do not care how taboo this is.
You are the only one I wanted.
You are the only one I needed.
Now you can just do away with yourself.

To place your lips on mine,
It must disgust you.
My heart would always skip a beat whenever I saw you.
I am sure you had the same feeling just once.

Just once in your life,
Why can you not go along with it?
I wanted to sink into you.
You were so warm.
You welcomed me for a while at least.

Are you afraid of me?
Are you afraid of this little taboo of ours?
Our hearts were once connected as one.

We evolved.
What is so evil about that?

You did not love me,
Did you?
You are constantly trying to avoid me,
Are you not?
Who is who now?
What is what now?

I know this love of ours is taboo.
I know this love of ours is forbidden.
Society can stuff a sock in it.
Society is going to burn in Hell anyway.

Why not give up?
Why not give in?
Your heart grows colder by the moment,
I am sure.
You get harder by the moment as well,
I am sure.

If you cannot accept yourself,
Why do you not do away with yourself?
What is the point of living?

To accept yourself is our freedom.

I wanted to be with you forever.
You are as beautiful as they come.
Your attitude about this is what makes you ugly.
You have grown ugly enough for me to want to shatter you.
I want to throw shards of glass at you.
I want to slice you open.
I want to see your blood.

I do not care who comes looking for you.
I do not care who comes looking for me.
I shall avenge your death by taking my own life.
Am I being too serious?

You have broken me in many ways.
I do not think even you realize.
I bear my heart to you.
All you do is give up on me.

This is a weird fantasy poem.
Of course, this is a weird fantasy poem.
Why would you think otherwise?
I know it is not real.
Do you not know it is not real?

This poem I write about you has emotion behind it.
Does that make it real?
Perhaps to some.
It depends on the imagination of one person.
You are the one who does not think.
You spew words regardless of what another feels.

Are you going to do away with yourself now?
Are you a coward?
If you are a coward,
You need to claim yourself and your label.

Are you brave?
If you are brave,
You need to stand up.
You need to stand up for what is right.
You need to do away with this ugly attitude of yours instead.
Instead of doing away with yourself,
You need to stick by my side like a real lifeline.

Don't Forget Her

The heartstrings play a soft melody.
It may be out of tune,

It may lay itself all over the place.
However, it is a tune, nonetheless.

See how she closes her eyes.
See how she sings her long-winded notes.
It is all under a breath.
There is just so much that she can sing.

The right tune.
The wrong tune.
It doesn’t matter.
Her heart beats with such loneliness either way.

Tune of dark,
Struggling to find the tune of light,
Her heart just can’t seem to find what it needs.
People here and people there,
Nothing seems to matter anymore.

Her silhouette is what remains of her.
Like a house laid away to be put to rest,
She has been fully gutted.
Her tired feet continue to search.

She trembles as she falls onto her knees.

Tears stream along her face.
They mix with the dirt, blood and sweat.
She can barely stay upright.

What a sad tune she sings.
She sings this tun with all her might.
Why doesn't anyone hear?
No one listens.

She's growing older by the second.
Her heart may very well freeze over,
Becoming increasingly cold.
"I deserve it," she tells herself.
"I deserve the misery I get."

See how she goes.
She her footsteps roam the barren wasteland.
She's not even wearing any shoes.
Her feet appear bruised and bloody and full of dirt.

Her search for the lighter tune continues.
It is all she can do.
The child in her arms laughs and plays.
Little does he know,
Little innocent thing,

She is suffering in silence.
Little does he know,
It is him.
That is the reason she lives.

“Misery always welcomes me,” she reminds herself.
“I’ve done bad things and now I’m paying the price.”
Her sins are stamped to her forehead,
Stamped to her aching heart.
“It’s what I’ve done.”

Her words,
Sharp as a knife,
Pierce the veil of black sky.
Her words,
Screech beyond her ears.
No one can hear her.
No one is willing to listen to her woes.

“Everyone has grief. Mine is nothing special,” she tells herself.
It’s what occurs to her constantly.
“I’m not that important.”
Like a leaf drifting in the wind,
She has detached herself.
Importance isn’t a thing anymore with her.

She’s been kicked around.

She’s been beaten.

Her entire body is just one big bruise.

As she lays dying,

Breathing her final breaths,

The blood seeps through her clothes.

It’s starting to finally return to the dirt in which it came,

Feeding the nearby trees.

That’s what she’s wasted to.

Finally, her eyes open and she breaths one final breath.

She lays there,

Staring up at the sky,

Her final light fading out.

Her dignity and humanity have returned to the earth.

It is all buried away,

Just like her aching heart,

It is all buried far away.

Erase

I wish I could turn back time.

I want to go back.

I want to return and stop myself.

I made one of the biggest mistakes in my life.

Now you want nothing to do with me.
Even that fact doesn't hurt.
What hurts is that I could ever have done that to you.
I feel like such a monster.

I feel like I shouldn't exist.
I've hurt you in the worst possible way.
I want to erase.
I want my memories to disappear.

I want to scream until the orbs in my brain shatter.
I want them to shatter into a million pieces.
I've tried to connect with you once again.
I know I should never have.

Why can't I let go?
Why can't I shove it all away?
I feel like I'm going crazy.
I know I have no right to feel what I'm feeling.

I know you've moved on.
I know I should move on.
I thought I had.

Maybe I was wrong.

You don't deserve the suffering.
It's myself who deserves whatever I've got coming.
You deserve better.
I don't deserve you.

Let me go.
Please, let me go.
I want to leave my memories locked away.
My soul aches.

Erase these memories.
Erase these emotions.
I hate seeing this.
I hate feeling this way.

We pass each other on by.
We don't say a single word.
You ignore me.
It's as if I don't exist.

It's okay.
I need things to be this way.
I was a monster.

I was a fool.

I wanted to be loved.
Even if it was by you,
I wanted so desperately to be loved.
I pushed too far and this is what I got.

Please, erase these thoughts from my mind.
I'm afraid I'm losing it.
I'm losing what I haven't already lost.
Get rid of this urge to push even more.

Erase what's going on with me.
This is territory that's off limits.
Every ounce of me yearns to enter.
Please, erase all of it.
I don't need any of it.
I don't want to suffer anymore.

Fated End

Do I care?
Do you care?
We all used to care so much.
Now we do not seem to care all that much.

Why is that?

I am evil.
I am mean spirited.
I can say the same about you.
Are you lonely like this?
I know I am.

Why can't we live together as one spirit being?
I do not think it all that bad.
Just follow me.
You would like very much for me to follow you instead.

I know what we are.
We are no longer individuals.
We fly into the skies above as two coming together as one.
I do not know why I contradict things so.

My mind is a bunch of random mess.
Why not help me straighten it out?
Just a little bit will do.
It is not up to me or you.
It is up to the both of us together and the higher powers of this world.

The world is cruel.

Prepare yourself for your long and agonizing journey.
Tongues will rip you apart limb from limb.
People will always shatter your heart.
They shattered mine and yours.

Do not try and fight it.
Sink into it and accept it.
You will find no salvation.
It is no wonder we have not died by now.

Do not try and save me.
Save yourself.
Maybe you will make it out alive.
I do not care if I perish trying to do whatever.

Do not come and seek me out.
I will not come and seek you out.
Remember that we are not one and yet we are not individuals.
Hold this inevitable fact close to your heart.

At last, we meet our end.
It is an end we cannot fight off.
It is an end so pleasing.
Now it is time to drift into a world of sparkling lights.

We are fate.
We are our own end.
It is done by our own hands.
Do not try and take it for granted.
We so often take it all for granted.

My footsteps are being smothered by yours.
I cannot take your wild emotions any longer.
I am raw as can be from the haunting scraping of one another.
My throat has screamed its last.

Blood now surrounds us as we lie together.
This end cannot be avoided in the least.
I have no more money.
You have no more money.
I am bare naked and so are you.

We have stopped holding hands long ago.
It has been so long since you uttered to me three sweet words.
Three sweet little words can mean so much.
Now we meet our end.
Yet we go on living for all of eternity.

This end will not be an end forever.
Actually, it is meant for us to travel from one world to another.

We are meant to cycle on.

I am you.

You are me.

It does not matter by which you and I call each other.

The time goes on and on.

It is never ending for us.

I will never fade even as I die.

You will never fade even as you die.

We will be together yet not together.

Gossip

Some of you may think I am that same person.

That same person from high school or from college,

The one who was so naive.

No, I am not.

Some of you may think I married a black man.

Some of you may think I had his baby.

Some of you may think I am super sexually active.

Some of you may think I am pregnant again.

Some of you may think I have four children.

When will it ever end?

This cycle of gossip needs to stop.

Gossip is only as good as gossip gets you into trouble.
Gossip is gossip.
Gossip is harmful.
Do not gossip.

I am not some dumb little girl.
I am told I was seen at this time and at this place.
No, I was not there and not at that time.
Stop the gossip.

I do not care who you are.
I do not care where you are in life.
Gossip is gossip whether it is out of harm or out of concern.
Do not stick your nose in my business.
You are not helping.

I do not know who you think you are.
Stop talking about me.
Stop this cycle.
It is not right.

The cycle of gossip is harmful no matter what.
I am not the painted picture in your mind.

I am not someone to be messed with so.
I am who I am, and I am no one else.

Let us get one thing clear now.
The gossip you take such pride in is incorrect.
I am not that person.
I am my own person.
I am who I make myself out to be.

I refuse to cave on this matter.
I have nothing against anybody.
Just stop the chain of gossip.
The person you have in mind is someone else entirely.

Do not get me wrong on this.
It is not for you to decide.
It is for me to decide.
Shall I glue your lips shut for all of eternity?

God will see what you are doing.
God considers what it is that you are saying.
Speaking so ill of another is harmful.
Speaking so ill of another destroys.

Stop trying to make me into this person.

I have painted my own person.
I know who I am.
I know what I am.
Do not try and destroy the person in front of you.

You all are blind.
You all ache far too much for an earful.
It gets your heart racing.
The drama of someone else's life is not for your story.

I have my own things to bring forth into this world.
I am not on my own planet.
I am not going crazy.
It is you who keeps making up what you wish.
Gossip gets you stitches in the end.

I know of your jealousy.
I know you wish for my slow and agonizing demise.
Do not try and cut me down.
You will never win over on me.

Heart Bursting Forth

The young woman in me is turning tricks.
I feel myself soaring through the sky.

It does not matter who sees me.
I am here.
I am staying right where I am.

I feel safe and warm in His arms.
His embrace is one that welcomes me.
I am not kicked out.
I am not shoved to the side.
I am not placed in a corner.

He loves me for who I am.
I love him for who He is.
He is mysterious, but He brings no ill intent.
There are many questions I have for Him.
However, that does not mean I do not want Him.

The fact of the matter is,
I need Him in my life.
He is my rock.
He has grabbed me by the shirt and dragged me away from danger.
He has told me I had better get my butt back where it belongs.

He is not mean.
He is merely firm.
I need Him to be firm with me.

He never wavers.
I cannot spend my life believing in someone who wavers.
He calls me out when I am behaving idiotically.
I need someone like that.

Someone who is not afraid to point things out to me,
I need Him for all of this.
I am blind as can be.
I cannot spot dangers from miles away.

I need Him.
I need Him in my life.
If not, what have I got?
Am I willing to be alone?
Am I willing to live out there on that island?
If not, I cannot just turn my back on Him.

I do not make my own rules.
Only God Himself makes the rules.
I just live by them is all.
I live by them to a tee.

God is the one I need in my life.
I do not need random mankind making random demands.
I do not need to heed the outside noise.

I do not need to heed the noise inside of my head.
I belong to God.

I know my worth.
Do you know yours?
If not, you need to do some searching.
God Himself is who I need in my life right now.
I do not need to listen to all the cons and negatives.

I need to love myself.
God loves how he has made me.
I need to do the same.
I cannot be unmade.

Heart Strings

The heart is like guitar strings.
If you put too much stress on them,
They break, break, break.
Do not worry though.
I am okay, okay, okay.

I can see it in your eyes, eyes, eyes.
You are not okay.
You are hurt beyond belief.

Is there anything I can do, do, do?

We sing a sad, sad song.
Do these lyrics meet you now?
I am sorry if I have hurt you.
You make a fool, fool, fool of me.

Can we touch, touch, touch?
I so desperately want to hold your hand.
I cannot get over, over you.
Baby, oh, baby, why can you see me?

I want to see you, you, you.
Let us be one, one, one.
I feel like such a fool.
Oh, I feel like such a fool.

I have lost your love, love.
Baby, I have lost your love.
"It is over," you say, say, say to me.
"I am so over you."

My love is greater than any you have ever had.
Your eyes sparkle in the night sky.
I look up to the moon, moon, moon.

Baby, why can you not see me?

Baby, I am still so into you, you, you.
I cannot seem to let go.
This love is forbidden I know.
Just listen to the stereo of my heart, heart, heart.

I feel like I am your fool, fool.
Let these words echo deep inside.
"I need you in my life," I say, say, say to you.
"I cannot live without you."

Baby, you have broken me, broken me several times over.
In the next life,
I will still be chasing after you.
Sacrifice I do, do, do.

I am ready to make nice.
If it is only to see you,
Baby, I am ready to make nice.

"COME BACK TO ME," I shout, shout, shout.
I need your lips on mine.
I am wasting away just waiting for you.
My voice is drowning in the storm.

I need you, you, you in my life, in my life.
Despite the heartache you cause me,
I need you in my life.
You are the only one.

I belong to you.
I am yours.
Please, be mine, be mine.
Let us go all the way, all the way into the night.
Leave me breathless with the way you do me, do me.

Baby, do you not see me?
This is my heart, my heart.
I miss you so bad, so bad.
What do I do without you?

This is my heart, my heart, my heart.
I need you here by my side, by my side, baby.
I miss the way you talk to me.
I miss all your sweet nothings.

If I were to die, to die tonight,
What would you do?
I would watch over you from heaven.

The flowers in my heart,

Still filled with love, with love,

Continue to bloom even more.

Last night, I thought about you, about you.

The truth is, I cannot let you go.

The tears stream out like a river of sorrow, of sorrow for your missed love.

Into the darkness is all I can see.

Where is the light?

My heart beats for you, you, you.

Is it too difficult for you to see?

This is just like a breakup song.

I feel about a million miles away from the world.

I drift alone forever, forever.

I Am Not Good Enough

Nothing I do feels good enough.

Just who am I living for?

I am not doing this for myself, am I?

I rely on an audience.

When I see people and what they have created,

I feel so lost.

I feel so alone.
I am drifting in outer space.

I am not good enough for me.
I think that is the way I feel.
When I am finished with a few things,
I sigh and close my eyes.
I imagine a world where I am good enough.

Do not take me for granted.
Who am I kidding?
I take myself for granted.
What I do,
What I say,
None of it is good enough for me.

I am just one person.
I have no advertisement when it comes to me.
I show genuine fun.
In reality,
I feel like nothing is good enough to show off.

When it rains,
It pours,
Just like it is raining cats and dogs outside right now.

I hate this.
Why can I not get over this?

What I do,
What I say,
None of it is good enough for me.
I cannot shout things to the world.
It takes too much energy.

I am not sure of myself.
I have lost all confidence.
The stupid seems to be the winner.
The sensible seems to be the loser.

I am not of myself.
I do not take away enjoyment from others.
I take it all away from myself.
I am a monster to myself.
For those who do not understand,
I am a monster to others.

All of this,
None of it,
Not an ounce of it is good enough.
I am not good enough.

I do not understand myself.

I am weathered and worn.
I have had enough.
My thoughts of not being good enough,
They refuse to leave me be.

These words repeat themselves.
I am not good enough.
I am not good enough for anything.
I am not good enough for anyone.
I hate this.

Do I not like what I do?
That is not what I am talking about.
I am not good enough.
I am just not good enough.
No one sees what I do.
I reach no one with what I do.
I am not good enough.
I am not good enough even for myself.

I Do Not Like You

You make me want to scream my head off.

I do not like you.
You are the cause to the fire in my eyes.
These flames of revolution are being flamed.

I do not like you.
Every bone in my body does not like you.
You put all your eggs in one basket.
You expect me to give it all up.

Do not expect me to fall for your charm.
I do not care how my garden is ripe.
I refuse to pick out of it right now.
That is way too fast.

Do not talk down to me.
I am not a little kid.
You should know by now that I am a woman.
I do not like you.

Just go away.
Stop kissing my butt.
You think I will let you in my front door.
Do not show up on my stoop.

I do not like you.

I do not like you.
Get this fact through your thick skull.
Why do you want me so much anyway?

I am not that young girl you met ages ago.
I have grown.
I have left many a fool behind.
I am not mad.

I do not know why you chase your tail so.
Are you up for fighting?
We are always up for fighting for anything.
Are we not?
Well, you can quit fighting for me.

Leave me to dwell within myself.
I will remain like this for the rest of my days.
My words make no sense.
I realize that.
It is up to you to bring these words to life.

I leave the meaning up to your heart.
Just know that I do not like you.
I do not like you.
Stop trying to strip yourself of who you are.

I am not compatible.

You must be sick in the head to get with me.

I am not going to wash your laundry.

I am not going to feed you.

Do not make me.

I will not have your baby either.

I do not like you.

What will it take for you to know this?

Stop shredding yourself of who you are.

It is for my sake I know.

This is nonsense.

My words are usually far and few.

However, these words have been brought to my heart.

I do not like you.

Quit trying to get me.

You are constantly chasing your thoughts.

Chase them down with some alcoholic beverage instead.

I do not like you.

Why do you keep chasing?

Go take a chill pill.

You think that you know me.
I think that you are dead wrong.
I do not like you.
I am not at all like you think I am.
I am not easy.
You are not easily chased off.
I do not like you.
That is all there is to it.

I Hate That

Shrouded in darkness,
This emptiness refuses to leave me.
No matter how much I try to hide it,
I know what I've done.
In spite of what you've told me,
I know I'm not forgiven.

I stand in front of the wreckage.
I've left quite a trail.
Even though I yearn for you with all my might,
I know you're gone for good.
Maybe I'm still in love with you.
I've questioned it before.

I hate that you hate me.
I don't want to live this life anymore.
It's grown boring.
There's nothing left of me.
You've ripped it all out.

I hate this so much.
I want to scream my heart out.
I want to cry myself dry.
I know this won't bring you back to me.
I know my actions have turned you away from me.

I hate that you hate me with all of your being.
After all that we've been through,
You no longer want me as I still want you.
My heart aches a great deal.

My very being is shedding tears for you.
I pray that you'll one day return to me.
My feelings aren't so special to you.
You've made this obvious.

Shall I pry out my eyeballs for you?
Do you want me to sever my guts?
I want to shred myself from the inside out.

If it's for you,

I'll do it.

You've made yourself clear.

You want nothing to do with me.

Have I made myself clear?

Do you know that I yearn for you?

After all this time,

Why can't you just accept it?

I don't get why I feel this way about you.

I can't have you.

You've made it obvious.

I need to stop now.

This is starting to become unbearable.

Please, won't you save me?

Please, I'm begging you.

Why won't you come to my rescue?

Are you that mad at me?

I hate that things have to remain this way.

We've made quite a rocky path.

We've got quite a rocky existence of one another.

You've erased me from your mind forever.

This is something I just cannot do.
This is something I've tried.

In A Mood

Sometimes you can hear me holler from miles away.
Maybe it is something you said to me.
It could be something you said about me.
Maybe it is something you did to me.

Sometimes I press my hands against my ears.
It is not the right time for this.
I do not want to hear you.
The melody you sing to me is a sad one.

Sometimes I squeeze my eyes shut.
The world is obnoxious.
Everyone and everything is annoying me.
I do not want to step foot in this life.

Can you not see?
I do not want to deal with the likes of you.
I may never want to deal with the likes of you.
You always stress me out.

Can you not see?
The topic you have chosen for me is mute.
It is stupid.
I want to complain as loudly to you as possible.

You are the one being stupid here.
I am the one being sensible for once in my life.
Sometimes I really come to hate your guts.
Sometimes I want to strangle you.

You will be the death of me.
Maybe you will meet your end by my own hands.
Why have I chosen you?
I can no longer choose you over anything.

I do not understand.
I am so underrated as a human.
No one cares.
I have quit caring myself.

It has been years since I have put myself first.
I have always been the first one to be eaten alive.
My emotions swirl wildly.
Can you not read the words on my lips?

You are annoying and so am I.
So what?
What is your point in the matter?
Our voices create a loud clatter when put together.

Maybe we will be as one in the next world.
Do not count on it though.
I hate you now.
I will hate you for all of eternity.
It is in the way you treat me.
It is in the way you no longer hold me tight.

Why can you no longer protect me from these thoughts?
You see me the way I am.
You know what a sad melody my heart sings.
My heart aches.
I long for you.
Hold me.
Love me.
Protect me.
Do not shame me.

What is your deal?
I am in a mood right now.
I am in no mood for fooling around.

I am sick of it all.
I want to throw it all away.
You are the center of this mess.
You can just exclude me from now on.

I do not get you.
Obviously, you do not get me.
I am not in the mood for joking.
This is not a laughing matter.
Please, leave me.
Just leave me.
Leave me right now.

I am no longer in the mood for you.
You have stressed me out enough.
You have depressed me enough.
I now hate you.
I will probably go on hating you.
We can make sweet hatred together.

Just One Step Away

I am barely hanging on.
I feel just one step away from losing my mind.
Only a ghost of my previous self continues to exist.

I do not know where my spirits have wandered off to.

I know not what I do or say.
I understand myself the least.
I am just one step away from losing my mind.
Let us just go ahead and end the suffering here.

It is driving me crazy that I cannot speak my mind.
I cannot speak my mind because my words refuse to come forth.
I honestly do not know what causes this.
This is a complete and utter mystery to me.

Can someone help me figure this out?
Can someone save me from myself?
The words are just itching to get out.
My throat is scratchy in my efforts to keep it all inside.

I want a scream to rip my throat out.
I want my meat and bones to show.
I want to be completely exposed.
I am truly afraid of it all.

I am a clueless jerk.
I know not how to behave.
The ways of my heart are a maze.

This is just how I am.

What you see is what you get.
The real me refuses to show.
I want it that way, yet I do not want it that way.
I maybe would like to keep people guessing.

I lie just to get by.
I lie straight through my wilding grinning teeth.
My lips utter all lies and not an ounce of truth.
I like to think I am not like water.
I do not know, but maybe I am like water.

Someone save me from myself.
Someone come to my rescue.
I want to find myself.
I want to know who I really am.

There are different versions of me.
I am one step away from losing myself.
The world has taken over me.
I am no longer of morals or injustices.

I no longer care about anything.
I know I should care more than I do.

I am just one step away from losing it all.
I have been tossed about.

I am all banged up.
My guitar strings are broken.
I can no longer sing my heart out.
I want to, but I no longer can get a word out.

Someone come to me.
Someone appear and save me from myself.
I am wandering around a world full of nothing.
I am trapped inside of my head.

I am just one step away.
Nothingness has kidnapped my heart.
My heart may never see the light of day.
Everything may never turn back to normal.
I am just one step away from losing everything.

I do not care and yet I do care.
I have become more and more lifeless over the years.
Life has been cruel to me.
Love has been cruel to me.
I want to get away from it all, yet I care way too much.

I cannot stand for the way I feel and yet I just allow it.

I am here and yet I am in another world.

It is a world of my own making.

I am just one step away from losing my sanity.

I am just one step away.

I lose it all and yet I make it all up.

Maybe I can do both.

To lose is to fade away.

I am just one step away.

I am just one step away from losing my sanity.

I cannot help it.

I wish I could just let it all out.

I never want to return here.

Key

The key to someone's heart.

What is that?

What is the key to someone's heart?

Is it expensive?

Is it cheap?

Is the key to someone's heart light?

Is it dark?

What about both?

What color is it?

Brown or red?

What shape does it take?

Is it in the shape of a key?

Is it in the shape of a heart?

Only God knows the key to someone's heart.

Only God knows what makes someone.

It's only God who can lead the way.

It's only God who can show us the key.

This is an overwhelming resolution to everything.

Why does this solve everything?

Why can't I solve things with my own hands?

Only God knows the answer to this question.

God holds the keys to everything.

So why not God show us the key?

It's only logical.

Know Versus Feeling

I can if I want to.

I'm smart enough to do so.
What's holding me back?
I need to climb out of this mess.

I've created the debris behind me.
I'm not perfect by any means.
I know the truth.
I refuse to acknowledge what's in front of me.

I can do it.
If I put my mind to it,
I know I can do it.
What if I'm not willing?

I'm stripped to the core.
I can't explain it.
This feeling inside rages its beautiful flames of destruction.
Please, continue to work on me.

I refuse to give up on myself.
I keep on trying.
I'm beaten and bruised.
I know what's going on.

Please, don't judge me.

I'm fully conscious of it.
I feel like I'm never good enough.
I know I'm good enough.

What I know and what I feel are two different things.
I want to be perfect.
I hate the reflection in the mirror.
I hate it so much.

I know I don't need to hate myself so much.
I already know this.
Despite what I know,
It doesn't align with how I feel.

I'm always on trial for something.
I'm always in trouble for one thing or another.
I work hard and I play hard.
Why do I feel like I can't catch my breath?

Life is full of vile things.
I'm the one in control.
I can pray all I want.
It is up to me to make the choice.

I need to get better than this.

I need to make it all known to me.
I can't feel this way forever.
I have to love myself eventually, right?

I want to be the model.
I'm already the actress.
All I do is smile.
I don't shed a single tear.

This is a story I want to complete the right way.
I don't want it to end like a tragic horror.
I'm not Juliet.
I'm not going to die just for a man's approval.

I know who I am.
I know what I'm capable of.
I'm desperate for approval.
I don't feel like I'm enough for anyone.

I can do this task.
I'm already beautiful.
I can't keep on hating the reflection in front of me.
I'm torn up inside, but I behave as if I'm alright.

I get it.

I understand.
I feel otherwise.
I'm smart enough to pull myself through onto the other side.

I need to fight.
I can't give in.
I need to do this.
I have others riding on my choice.

Leave It Be

Let it go.
Let it lie.
It's no use.
Don't fight it.

Love will find you right where you stand.
Let it be.
Leave well enough alone.
If you push,
Love will be rushed.

It's not your season yet.
You've got the most beautiful miracle.
You should be content with that.

Don’t be so quick to get right back to it.

Close your eyes.
Take a deep breath.
Let the wind carry you along.
Let the fresh, cool water wash over your soul.
What’s good of love when it’s rushed?

Don’t lose your temper.
Love isn’t always timely.
Have patience.
Love will find you.

Stop trying to search with your eyes.
Look with your heart.
Love will always find you.
It doesn’t matter where you are.

Attraction can’t be forced.
Allow yourself to know,
You’re beautiful inside and out.
Don’t let others tell you otherwise.
Now is not the time to fall in love.

Just because someone isn’t right there beside you,

Just because all the wrong people are saying, “I love you,”
Doesn’t mean that you’re of any less value.
You think that maybe if someone were coming to you,
At your age,
That there must be something wrong with that person.
Not necessarily so.

Just like dreams,
Wishes are free and scarring.
Don’t entirely lean on what you want.
Just because you want it,
Doesn’t mean you’re going to get it.
Still, don’t stop fighting for what you want.
Just don’t be sore when you’re lead to something else entirely.

Leave it be.
Allow life to pull you along on the rollercoaster ride.
Let your drama have many seasons.
Allow people to see you for who you are.
Don’t stop the adventure short.
Don’t call it off.

Leave it be.
Stop trying so hard.
You’re a people pleaser to the point it’s unhealthy.

If a guy doesn't like you,
He really means it.
Settle for being friends.
If he doesn't even want that,
Turn your back and walk away.

Let It Be Free

I must learn to stand up on my own two feet.
Love and respect for myself is also a must.
I can't always rely on a man.
I need to rely on myself and God.

Men are starting to become total headaches to understand.
I'm not just some slut you can push around.
I'm not easy either.
Don't let my behavior fool you.
I'm smarter than I let on.

Just because I'm single,
Just because I don't have a man in my life,
That doesn't give you permission to chase me down.
Every single fool on this earth will probably chase me down.

I'm being more aggressive than usual.

Surprised?
Don't be.
I'm not your fool to take and control.

I get frustrated when a guy doesn't pay attention to me.
However, I want the right guy to pay attention to me.
Don't get me wrong on this.
I'm not here to mess with anyone's head.

Men do so enjoy looking desperate.
Yeah, you there, in front of me.
I'm referring to you.
Stop trying to chase me down.

Let me slow down.
Let me close my eyes and breathe.
I have loads of questions to ask myself.
I've lost bits and pieces of myself.

Everything isn't as it was.
What I thought was turns out to be the exact opposite.
More questions are pouncing at my door.
I realize none of this makes sense.
It all makes sense to me though.

What do you make of me?

What do I make of myself?

Why can't I stop talking like this?

Life and love.

It's all just one big, complicated riddle.

Let it be free.

Let me be free.

Don't mess with things too much.

I may or may not lose interest.

You've probably lost interest in me by now.

I've scared many a man off.

I don't care.

See what you want to see.

I need to be free to be who I am.

Little Doll

Little doll hands,

So stained with blood,

So much so that her own tears cannot blur it out.

It does not matter how much she scrubs,

She will never rid herself of the past.

Little doll eyes,
All has been seen.
Nothing can be unseen.
Crimson red blood even seeps from her sockets.

Little doll heart,
One that is so broken,
It cannot be put back together again.
Many have tried.
None have succeeded.

Little doll spirit,
Something so shattered,
Something no longer there,
It cannot be revived.
Many have tried.
None have succeeded.

Her little doll screams,
Ones that cannot be heard,
Ones that fade away with distance,
She will never live to tell her story.

Little doll ears,
Ones that hear the world scream at her.

No one likes profanities.

Not even her.

Little doll,

Little doll,

One who cannot cope.

There is always one who sims in her own blood,

As well as someone else's,

She is the only one left it seems.

Little doll,

Little doll,

She is not the enemy!

She just wants revenge for the wrongs done to her.

Watch out.

She might come for you next.

She has taken the sharpest knife,

Taken it to her flesh,

Taken it to someone else's,

She has always had a need for such objects.

The world says she is a freak.

The world refuses to cope with her.

She takes up a needle,

A needle to sew her life back together,
An object to sew a nice and neat story,
Happy endings galore!

The little doll feels she is old and worn.
She is falling apart at the seams.
No one knows.
No one cares.
She is the only little doll in the world.

She is a flawed little doll.
No one wants her.
No one wants to hug her.
No one wants to give her kisses.
It is because she is out of date.

She no longer has the fashion she once did.
The little doll she is,
The little doll she refuses to be,
It all runs together.
Part of her wants it.
Part of her does not want it.

Little doll,
Little doll,

Grasp at your happiness.

No matter what,

If they want you,

They will be willing to sacrifice themselves.

That is just the way it is.

Lonely Flow of Time

Lonely girl in the corner,

Looking so pitiful with her big blue eyes.

She feels she has lost something of internal value.

Like a shattered clock,

She's broken deep inside.

She needs love.

However, out of fear,

She fully rejects that love.

Will someone raise a voice to her?

Will someone raise a hand to her?

"I deserve this," she says to herself.

"I deserve to be punished for the sins I have committed."

What sins were those?

She closes her eyes with a sigh and shakes her head.

"It doesn't matter. I know I have committed quite a bit of sin."

She knows she can be forgiven.
“I refuse to forgive myself,” she says.
“Why are people so kind to me?”
She isn’t ungrateful.
In fact, it touches her soul deeply.

“I’m not good enough,” she says.
She feels she doesn’t deserve kindness or happiness.
“All I deserve is misery.”
She wills the pain to come at her full force.

Her fears have become her reality.
She knows nothing more than that.
Things have been taken away from her.
She is the only one to blame.

Her emotions stand in her way.
There is always a way to get better.
“I dare not touch such a thing,” she tells the world around her.
Is there anyone who can beat this?
Can it be her?

The lonely girl in the corner may never win.
At least she will die trying.

It’s always a fight.
“How much longer can I endure this,” she wonders aloud.

She opens her eyes,
Staring straight out in front of her,
Realizing the world around her.
“Am I seeing through blurry lenses,” she asks herself.
Maybe what was in front of her wasn’t all there was to be.

She shook her head.
“I can change,” she tells any ear willing to listen.
The hands of time will wring her neck if she keeps this up.
“Tik tok, tik tok, time rushes forward forever,” she can’t help but say.
There was nothing else left of her.
The hands of time wrench her forward by her neck.

“I can’t stand here in this place forever.”
That was something even she knew.
“I’m frozen in time. I’m broken.”
While everyone else moved forward,
She stood in place,
Something she knew all along was trouble.

“I need to piece myself back together somehow.”
She knew this all along.

“I have to put one foot in front the other.”

Nothing ever came easy to her,

She knew.

However, she also feels herself floating through time.

“Time always moves forwards. Never backwards.”

Lonely Girl Lonely Boy

“Say, won’t you die with me,” asks a lonely girl up on the rooftop.

“Why do you want to die,” asks the lonely boy in response.

The lonely girl laughs.

“What?”

“Come on. Don’t tell me you haven’t come up here for the same reason as I.”

“You know this is wrong, right?”

The lonely girl shrugs.

“I don’t care,” she says.

“Don’t you have someone or something to lose?”

The lonely girl shakes her head.

The lonely boy sighs.

A smile creeps across his lips.

It is just a ghost of a smile.

It is a smile all the same.

The lonely girl,
Standing on the ledge of the eighteen story building,
Says to the lonely boy, “Do you?”
The lonely boy steps up onto the ledge,
Standing beside the lonely girl,
Taking her by the hand.
He squeezes her hand gently.

“Don’t try and talk me out of this,” she says to the lonely boy.
“It’s your choice,” says the lonely boy,
His voice casual.
“You act like this is an everyday thing for you.”
“Well, it’s not,” answers the lonely boy.

“Are you going to die with me?”
“That depends,” says the lonely boy.
The lonely girl gets frustrated and begins to glare at the lonely boy.
“Shut up before I throw you off this ledge!”
“That would be a murder suicide,” answers the boy.
His expression turns smug and so does his voice.

“ARE YOU KIDDING ME,” howls the lonely girl.
“I can tell that you’re fed up with me,” responds the lonely boy.
“Gee, what gave you that idea,” the lonely girl says.
Her voice is sarcastic.

The boy laughs hard.

"WHAT IS SO FUNNY," the lonely girl snaps,
About ready to shove him off the ledge,
About to allow herself to go right behind him.
"I see I've gotten under your skin," the lonely boy tells her.

He pulls her close.
She feels his warmth breath on her ear.
Realizing what is happening,
Her heart skips a beat.
Heat rises into her face.
"Could this be love," the lonely boy whispers,
His lips brushing her ear.

The lonely girl pulls away and slaps a hand over her ear.
She glares at the lonely boy,
Thinking for just a moment.
"I'm not in the mood anymore," she tells the lonely boy.
The lonely boy's eyes light up.

"What's it to you," the lonely girl snaps at the lonely boy,
Though her voice now more quiet,
Though her intentions now less severe.
"It's you, isn't it," the lonely boy says.

Two lonely hearts join as one.
On the rooftop,
Way late at night,
Where no one is to bother them.

“Why did you do it,” the lonely girl asks.
“It was well worth it,” the lonely boy responds.
“Shut up,” the lonely girl snaps,
Feeling a sense of embarrassment.
“Tomorrow, I’ll definitely do it,” the lonely girl tells the lonely boy.
“You’re pushing your luck,” the lonely boy tells her,
Collecting her in his warm embrace.

“You’re so fragile,” the lonely boy says.
The lonely girl gently shakes her head.
She tires of fighting with him.
“Yeah. Sure. Whatever,” she simply tells him in the end.

Lonely Heart

I stare out the window and watch the cars and trucks pass on by.
Say, have you ever had this sudden strong feeling to skip town?
Right then, that’s exactly what I was thinking.
I wanted to board the nearest bus or train.

Maybe I could have just driven until my car ran out of gas.
Maybe I could have walked the rest of the way.

The feeling gets so strong.
I think I'm about to cry.
Before I can shed a tear,
Before my thoughts can carry any further,
My plate of food I ordered arrives.

I keep thinking.
I keep thinking that this is my chance.
The only thing:
Do I keep this young one or do I let him go?
Don't get me wrong on this.
I love him dearly.
I would do or say anything for him.
I would even die for him.

Would I be just another mother who has abandoned her son?
Would things really be any worse?
What I mean is that he has no father.
The man who was his father,
That man,
He doesn't have any right.

There are times when I dream.
Why am I always running away?
Is there really something to be afraid of?
Why do I always insist upon climbing a fence or a tree?
Just what is it am I trying to run away from?

In my oddball dreams,
I always end up falling to my death.
I'm constantly being pushed over the edge of some cliff.
It's such a sad sight to witness.
What if it's inside of me?
What if it's not all that far off?

Maybe life is finally pushing me over.
It's always possible.
I need to stand up for myself.
I need to keep my footing.
If I don't,
If I fail,
I can't relive my life.

I don't know what to expect of myself.
I used to think I knew.
The awful truth is,
I've grown numb to understanding myself.

I’m always talking in riddles whenever I write.
It might be because I don’t understand myself.
I want to connect with others.
I want to bond through pain and happiness.
I want to share the burden.

Right now,
I feel alone.
I try and remember those who are dear to me.
It’s difficult trying to do all of this.
I tend to go through this cycle way too much.

There is this red ribbon around my heart.
The thorns grow more and more each time I think of this.
It’s awful.
There’s no one to share this with.
Of course, the world will read my words.
That’s not the same as close friends.
That’s different.
I’m bonded with the world through my words.
I’m not bonded with friends through my words.
I need the bond between myself and friends.
Don’t you agree?

My emotions can be a mess.
I'm not all that clean or worthy of much.
I may not be right or fair at times.
I try to be as kind as possible.

Love Hate

I try to reach out my hand to you.
I still fail every time.
Why won't you come back to me?
What makes you so afraid?

I've done everything.
I've been super nice to you.
What more could I possibly do?
The urges to slice through my flesh come strong.

I can't get what I want.
I don't get it.
Now I'm about to throw a fit.
I still don't get it.

It's cold.

I'm cold.
Even when it's hot out,
Even when the sun is shining,
I find it freezing.

Maybe I'm morbid.
I don't know.
Maybe I'm just a little bit psycho.
I don't know.
Maybe I'm just having a mental breakdown.
I don't know.

Why can't this go away?
These thoughts remain.
I'm punishing myself.
It's possible that I enjoy crushing my heart.

I didn't know I could seem so out of control.
My thoughts,
My emotions,
I feel like they are all bursting from the inside.
I don't know how much longer I can keep it up.

I’m obsessed over you.
I need you.
I want you.
I’ve got almost everything in my life.
It’s not enough.
I still want more.

I write the same things over and over again.
I slice through my flesh over and over again.
It’s all because of you.
I want to get rid of you.
If it weren’t for you,
If it weren’t for the words you said,
I wouldn’t be standing here.

I want to choke the life out of you,
Put my hands tightly around your throat,
Bruise your neck until it’s ugly.
The sight of it all is a pleasant one to me.

I love you.
I hate you.
I can’t make up my mind.

I feel love and hate at the same time.

Love Loss

I have fallen in love.
I have tried.
I have failed.
Quite the miserable one it was.

It is time to grow up.
It is time to put some hair on your chest.
Get that hair nice and thick.
Make it curly.

That thing between your legs must drop.
It must get bigger.
You must wear bigger underwear.
You are no more than a toddler right now.

I cannot afford you.
I cannot take in your negativity.
I refuse to wait on the sidelines for you to realize.
This is something I cannot tolerate.

I should not have to compete with video games.

Your affection should always be turned towards your family.

Do not insert your mother into the relationship.

Do not insert your cousin, brother, sister, so forth.

I cannot fight your battles as well as my own.

I am already a tree standing tall.

Stop trying to lean up against me.

I am not your life saver.

Only you can be yourself.

It is up to you to scat.

You know you do not have to take the manipulation.

You can fight.

I know you can.

Maybe you do not want to.

Pick yourself up.

Drag yourself with whatever part of your body works.

You have a heart.

You have a soul.

I know you do.

You have shown me once before.

My tears are your fault.

You are the cause of my broken heart.

I tried to love you.
We created a child together.

Are video games all you care about?
Is that the kind of life you wish to live?
You are in your own little world.
You are narrow.
Your mind cannot expand.
What is holding you back?

Your kid is inquisitive.
He is just like me.
He reminds people of you.
Why can you not see the beauty we have?

Your ways are foul.
You cannot keep a clean home.
You lay in your slop all day long.
You stay up with a blue light in your face.

It is time to wake up.
You are a living being.
You once made me feel things.
The electricity is now gone.
Does it have to be gone forever?

If you cry out of unfairness,
Remember that you are the one who has done me wrong.
If I find someone else,
It is your loss.
You had your chance.
You did not even try.
You blamed it all on me.

Mistakes that Make no Sense

You know?
There is this person I know of.
She is just waiting to be raped.
She is just waiting to be murdered.

Is she waiting for the last shoe to fall?
Is she waiting for the curtain to finally close?
Why does she desire the show to end so?

Sometimes I think she wants the life strangled out of her.
Sometimes I don't think she cares either way.
Maybe she will end up unlucky pregnant.
What will she tell the child?
"Welcome to the world! Your father raped me!"

I don't think she knows just how crazy she sounds.
This person isn't me.
This is someone else who wants to mirror me.
I have a doppelganger.

There is always someone who looks like me.
She is always wandering around town.
She continues to get lost.
It's like those many times in the past.

People don't care whether or not they have the right person.
All they want to do is accuse.
Maybe I did say something.
Maybe it was this girl who looks like me.

Many people think they've seen me.
We've never met.
Nope.
Not even once.
I think you've got the wrong person.

I'm tired of people thinking I'm a girl.
I'm not like the little girl who wanders around aimlessly.
I have someone.

I have someone besides myself for once in my life.

My heart is reflected in the mirror that is this life.
Maybe I've been playing around too much.
I sometimes like to toy with my prey.
So does this other person you all claim is me.

Did I go around getting pregnant throughout town?
No.
I don't even air out my dirty drawers for everyone to see.
This other person does.

I don't think people realize what is what with me.
I'm here and maybe I'm not.
Ever considered it?
Consider which one is actually me.

Am I talking to myself?
I may as well be.
No one ever listens to what I've got to say.
When I say it's not me,
I mean it's not me.

No one believes me.
I'm always punished for things I didn't do or say.

It’s not right.
It’s not fair.
I run around in circles for all of eternity.

Moving Forward

Like a withered sunflower,
Our love for one another has died.
You have become a big child.
You have problems.
Your baggage does not belong to me.

I thought you would straighten your way.
A promise you have made to me twice,
Twice now you have broken my heart.
You have destroyed me inside out.

You have turned me over.
My life is no longer to be shared with you.
You have proven all my love wrong.
You have proven society right.

You are a menace.
I am moving on with my life.
I do not care what you must spew.

Your word vomit means nothing to me now.

The gears in my mind and heart are moving forward.
I am leaving you behind.
The gap between us widens.
I do not reach for you anymore.

You need not come to me.
I do not want you back.
You can high tail it out of here.
I do not hate you.
I hate your bad habits.
Bad habits always die hard.

I should have known.
You are not expected to change.
You are expected to improve upon your character.
You have shown me naught.

The sun always shines through the clouds.
Even if it is a rainy day,
The sun always manages to shine through.
Even though you make me sad,
I will always have hope for other things.

It is time for bigger things.
It is time for better things.
I want to go to school again.
I want to move up in the world.

I do not need a man who refuses to make a little extra.
I need a man who will work for us to have things.
I need a man with a home.
I need a warm man to hold onto me.
I want to hold onto a warm man.

I do not need your petty attitude.
I need God in my life.
I do not need you to steer me away.
That is all you have done.

Not the Right One

You're not the right one.
You're not the right man for me.
You can't even stick around for the hard parts of life.
Let that sink into your mind.

All you want to do is fool around.
I'm not in the mood for your games.

You can't even make up your mind.
Do you want me or not?

When you don't get your way,
When something unexpected happens,
You want to run for the hills.
I'm not taking my clothes off for you.

I have told you before.
What did you think I was talking about?
You thought things wouldn't be so serious.
At least you hoped that I would be all yours.

Stop it.
Just stop it.
There is no sense in all that.
Just stop your processing right now.
You don't really know me.
You have no right to judge.

Why I do things,
Why I say things,
You have no right to tell me anything.
Don't even ask about it.

I tried to talk to you.
You wouldn't listen.
You're not the right one.
You're not the right man for me.

When things get tough,
If you don't get your way right away,
You run for the hills.
You can't even support me.

This is why you will be alone.
You can't handle things.
This is exactly why you will always be alone.
You will never have a girlfriend with your current attitude.

Stop looking for that perfect woman.
She doesn't exist.
You don't need me in your life.
I don't need you or your negativity in mine.
You only want what you want.

You claimed that you cared about me.
Oh please.
Don't make me laugh.
Is this you "caring" about me?

You even tagged the “no matter what” onto that.
Is this your “no matter what”?

All you do is point your finger at me.
All you do is judge me.
I am who I am.
I’m not perfect.
I struggle just like everyone else.

What is your dream woman anyway?
It most certainly isn’t me.
That’s obvious.
You block me and then you unblock me.
Who does that?

In my eyes,
In my heart,
You’re only on this planet to mess with me.
You’ve hurt me.
You’ve hurt me deeply.

Why do you blame me for my struggles?
That’s not fair.
Your heart is filled with nothing but darkness.
I should know.

I’m obsessed with it.

Path to Healing

I am smart.
I am beautiful.
I don’t have to work myself to death.
There isn’t anything to gain.

I’m on this path.
I’m headed in the right direction.
I feel it.
I feel so strong.

When God made me,
He didn’t make a mistake.
I need to stop caring so much about what others think.
I have to get my livelihood back somehow.

I’m prepared to fight my way out, tooth and nail.
I will claw until I bleed.
I won’t even stop there.
This will not destroy me.

I’m prepared to stand up and fight.

My life and so much more is on the line.
I have to fight this.
I cannot allow my demons to win.
If they win,
If they overcome me,
I won't be myself anymore.

I feel just a little bit stronger,
Sitting here,
Typing this up.
I feel just a little bit lighter.

My heart cannot stop singing words to heal me.
I know what I've got to do.
This is the hardest thing I've ever done.
To just sit here and let things be,
They are what they are.

Life is what I make of it.
I don't have to let my demons roam free.
I can control them.
God can help me.

Only I can do this.
With God's help of course.

I must make the decision to overcome this.
This isn't good for anyone involved.

I know I can do this.
I'm smarter than I let on.
I have to quit doubting myself.
While my struggles are a part of me,
They don't make me who I am.

It's okay to not be okay.
That doesn't mean I can't put up a fight.
No matter what,
I will always put up a fight.
It may sometimes be a pathetic fight.
It may sometimes be impeccably strong.

Savage Headspace

What am I?
Who am I?
Am I pretty?
Am I special?

I am impulsive.
I eat way too much.

I can be mean at times.
I am overwhelmingly nice at times.

When I feel like it,
I give hugs and kisses.
I do not know why.
I just cannot help myself.

I can be a pain in the butt.
I can behave myself.
There is no telling what you will get from me.
I am not so easily predictable.

My savage mindset is not to be so easily messed with.
I can be what I want.
It does not matter what is in my heart.
All the power is on me.

I can be someone's worst nightmare.
I can be something entirely unheard of.
My tongue never stops flapping.
The words I utter never cease.

There are times when I show off.
I show off to everyone I know.

I can shatter a stone-cold heart.
I can melt an ice-cold heart.

With my words,
With my actions,
You never know what you might get.
Am I a dream?
Do I really exist?

I dare to say these words.
No one can ever take these words away.
I can always be found.
No one ever loses me.

My will,
My spirit,
My soul,
None of it will ever be removed.
I do not care how much someone tries.
It cannot be gotten rid of.

Everything in this world seems the same to me.
Nothing ever changes.
Life goes on and on.
Will I die?

Will I live as well?

The life I knew is gone.
It is behind me.
That is where it will remain.
I am out of my cage of sin.

This savage state of mind is what I am now.
I cannot help it.
My heart was shattered.
My heart was put back together once more.
I will never be the same.

Things happen.
Maybe they happen for a reason.
People say what they do not mean.
We reach out to one another.
None of it matters anymore.

Seeking Redemption

I know I'm just being silly.
I know I need to let you go.
Why is this do difficult?
I'm always searching for you.

If you were to ever read this,
How would you react?
What would you say to me?
What actions would you take?
Knowing you and all your hatefulness,
You would probably block me.

You've blocked me out of everything enough.
Why can't you seem I'm seeking redemption?
I'm trying to get approved by you.
Why can't you just take a step back and see that?

Your words are cruel.
Your words are spoken by your silence.
I'm lost.
I'm lonely.
You were my last female friend.

Why must you continue to hurt me?
Don't you get what you're doing to me?
I know I'm stupid.
I know this whole poem is stupid.
I don't think I really care anymore.

I want to speak out loud to you.
Even if it's only by these words,
I want you to hear them.
I want you to heed every word I'm telling you.

I'm calling out to you.
I'm reaching my hand out to you.
Don't bite me.
Don't slap me away.
Don't leave me in this darkness.

Respond to me.
I don't care how you do it.
Just respond to me.
I want your approval.
I want redemption.

Stop trying to remain out of my reach.
My arms aren't long enough to reach you.
My legs aren't long enough to keep up with you.
I need you.
I want you.
Why don't you get that?

I'm seeking redemption.

I'm seeking acceptance.
Why are you so bent on killing me?
This is murder.
This isn't love at all.

I need to be loved by you.
I want to be loved by you.
It can't be anyone else.
I've already tried that.
I'm a freak to everyone else.
I guess now I'm a freak to you.

Society Complains About Being Single

"I've been single for years."
Have you ever wondered why?
Ask yourself that next time you decide to post on social media.
What are we?
We are human beings.
We are allowed to have emotions.

"I want a girlfriend. It's not fair that everyone else has one."
Not everyone has a girlfriend.
Check into what it is that you are doing with your life.
Are you too busy with your toys?

No, not sex toys!

Jeez, you people sure do have dirty minds!

"I want a boyfriend. Why don't I have one?"

Maybe you have a potential boyfriend.

Many guy friends often get 'friend-zoned'.

At least, that is what some people tend to call such a thing.

You do not want to mess up such a good friendship.

Okay, I get that.

However, meanwhile, stop complaining.

"Everyone else has somebody while I'm still single."

Not everyone has someone else.

If they do have someone else, I am sure they want to choke them.

Yes, I want to choke my husband sometimes.

He drives me crazy!

Oh, be quiet with the fact that I drive him crazy!

I am not speaking about us.

Oh wait.

I am.

Anyway, that is beside the point.

"I want to do music. I need a girl to stand by cheering me on."

Do you now?

Well, I have something for you.

What you want often goes on the backburner.

It does not matter how badly you want it.

If it takes up too much time and effort,

Throw it out the window.

The lot of you do not understand.

A lot of work goes into a relationship.

You cannot just run off to the gym.

First, feed and bathe your kid.

Make sure your kid has a clean diaper.

You come last.

When you have finally finished everything,

Are you tired?

Then, forget gym or music or writing!

It is time for you to get yourself to sleep.

You work early, right?

When you wake up,

You want to do your make-up, right?

Well, you will not always get to do this.

A lot of women out there have make-up and a baby on the hip.

These are women who have strict structure.

I mean, they get up almost three hours before their shift.

They do this every single day.

Some people attend class reunions.
Some people go out to party.
Where is your kid?
Oh right, with your parents.
Maybe social media is at fault for making this seem so.
Every single post I see about a woman with four kids,
Going out to party,
Yeah, what is with that?

It feels like us married women do not get help.
We are always the ones to pay for everything.
However, some of us refuse to be the victim.
The foolish go on having child after child,
Doing so when they know full well they cannot afford it.
Those women,
I have found,
Are the ones to get the help because they are single mothers.
This is just plain foolish.

Yes, I know!
This is yet another talk sort of poem.
Be quiet and deal with it!
I am talking and you need to be listening.

There are people who just do not get it.
They have thickened skulls.
Their brains have been taken over by terrible things.
Some just want to fool around.
Well, some of us are being serious.

It is okay to play video games.
It is okay to create music.
It is okay to write.
It is okay to go to the gym.
However, it is not okay for these things to take so much of your time.
Time management is something that needs to be learned.

Oh, be quiet, you!
Quit complaining because you get yet another lecture.
Am I really someone who knows nothing?
I think you had better consider things again.

It takes time and effort to even begin to date.
This is something I will one day teach my child.
I will teach all my children.
They will learn pretty quick that dating is not for everyone.

Sometimes a simple seizure can cause a breakup.
If you land yourself in the hospital,

The guy could get scared and run for the hills.
Money, sex, you name it.
To have a relationship, there is loyalty and commitment behind it.

White picket fence,
Big house,
Lots of children and animals,
Sweet neighbors,
Bright, sunny skies with a few clouds drifting by,
Not everyone gets that.
A lot of the time,
It is not like that at all.

Stop Taking Things For Granted

"I don't care."
"I don't want this."
"I'm not going to…"
Why do you take what you have for granted?
It makes me mad when all I hear are those words.
They spill forth from your lips so easily.

I want what you've got.
I can't have what you've got.
It's not fair.

You'd never hear me complain so.
I never ever complained when I had what you've got.

It enrages me so that all I hear from you are words I would never say.
Why would you not value what you've got?
I suppose the same could be said about me.
I've got the stress free tasks, right?
Wrong.
It's not stress free at all.

I'm one of the most socially awkward people you would ever meet.
Of course what I've got is just as stressful.
It may be even more stressful.
It depends on a lot of things.

I hate the way you express distaste at what you've got.
You've got what I've wanted.
You've got what I can't have.
Stop taking every single thing for granted.
Value what you've got right now.

Stop looking for excuses not to care.
Own up to your actions.
It may not matter to you.
It definitely matters to me.

Take the moments as you go.
Don't make excuses not to.
This is your life.
This is a task I want, but can't have.

Don't you get it?
Of course you don't understand.
You never understand me at all.
You think I'm just some lazy fool who doesn't care.
You think I've got a free ride in what I do.

I do what I do out of love.
I love what I do, but I want to take the next step upward.
It's something I want.
It's something I cannot have.
I may always want it, but never receive it.
What's not to get about that?

No one ever listens to me.
No one ever hears my voice.
There is this tune ringing inside of my heart.
It's in every fiber of my being.
It's in my very soul.

I'm not just some soulless freak like some of you think.
I have a heart.
I have a mind.
I'm not just some tool used for humanity.
You can't do with me whatever you like.
You can't say to me things with such disgust.

I know you don't like me.
You probably never will like me.
This doesn't mean you can treat me with such distaste.
I'm tired of the way I'm treated.
It's enough.
I've had enough.

I want to stand my ground.
I want to let you know things.
I'm not problematic.
Maybe you're the one who is problematic.
I don't go running my mouth like you do.
I don't claim that I'm useless like you do.
I can do what my heart tells me to do.
Just like that, I can do it just as much as you.

I feel things I can no longer hold back.
I feel things I want to bring forth into this world.

I cannot hold them down.

They boil up inside of me.

I want you to know what's up.

You can't just treat me the way you have been.

I don't like it.

Stop taking every single little thing for granted.

Do what you do.

Do it with heart.

Love it.

Live it.

Give it all you've got.

Don't come up with that negative attitude of yours.

Start caring.

Start doing.

Stop complaining.

My ears have heard enough.

My heart hurts for what I've heard.

It's not right.

It's not fair.

Tears is What is Left of Me

I look heavenward,

The heated water from the shower beating on my back.

Tears threaten to make themselves appear.
Funny thing,
I have not cried in a while.
It feels as if it has been years since I last cried.
What keeps holding me back?

I have this feeling welling up inside of me.
I am worthless.
I am useless.
I am powerless.
Otherwise, I do not know what or who I am anymore.

I am not worthy.
I do not deserve love.
I only deserve severe punishment.
Late at night,
The darkness rolls in.
The clouds look menacing.

My heart cannot keep up.
It cannot keep up with what is going on.
The stress of it all,
It is all just too much.
I feel myself going down.
I am being dragged down against my will.

I usually fight this off.
I am so used to standing on my own two feet.
I need to take some steps forward.
I cannot remain in this place.
If I do,
It will destroy me.

This is how I feel.
Then you look up at me with those star blue eyes.
All you need from me is my endless loving care.
You expect nothing else from me.

I like your innocent spirit.
It is because you have not been tainted by this world.
Just wait some more years.
You will probably hate me as well.
At least, you would push me away.

I do not know if I have it in me.
Do I have it in me?
Will I survive this urge?
Words cut deep like a knife into my flesh.
I bet I can carve the cruelness of my brain,
Carve it all over my body.

Will I meet my end?
Probably not.

I bet I will just suffer.
Keep on suffering through this I will.
Nobody sees the pain on the inside.
I hide it so well.

Money is money.
Heart is heart.
Debt is all I bring into this world.
Debt to everyone.
Debt behind everything I am.

I have nothing to my name.
Just my tears.
That is all I have.
Just my tears.
I hide them away.
I do not even hand them over.

What?
Are you expecting some witty saying?
Well, I have none right now.
All I have is the way I feel.

All I have are my endless tears.

I am screaming and crying on the inside.

I do not understand this life.

This is a life where everything goes wrong.

I pray to God for just one day to go right.

Not even God will answer me.

Not even God will save me.

God is more than likely to end me.

Temptation and War Inside

The brain doesn't see that she is beautifully and wonderfully made.

The brain tells her all the time that she's fat.

Sometimes the brain says, "You're fat. Do something about it."

Sometimes the brain says, "You deserve to be fat. You're going to remain fat."

She feels as if she's about to cry.

Her brain tells her, "Screaming, crying, whining and banging yourself up isn't the way."

"Just don't eat," her brain insists.

"I want the beans," she tells herself.

Her stomach growls.

"If you eat the beans, you'll get fat," her brain teases her.

"I want the cookies. Just a little won't hurt," she tells her brain.
"No. You'll get fat. You know how your body works," says her brain.
She says, "God made me. He wouldn't want me to do this to myself."
The brain says, "It doesn't matter."

"My body will shut down and I will die," she says.
"So? What's your point?"
It's like a war inside of her head.
Every single thought is filled with pitch black.

All she can see is darkness.
Jealousy has made its way into her heart.
"Why can't I look like that," she asks herself.
"I want to look like the pictures in front of me," she tells herself.

"Don't do it. Don't make people worry about you."
"That doesn't matter," her brain tells her repeatedly.
"Am I really just doing this for attention," she questions herself.
"Even if that is your motive, what of it?"
She squeezes her eyes shut and shakes her head vigorously.

A heated blush comes over her.
She pictures a man in her head.
The more she takes hold of the man,
The more she sees.

The more she sees,
The more she feels herself tighten up all over.

She can see her heated breath.
She struggles not to hold her breath.
"No! This isn't right," she scolds herself.
"Of course, it isn't right, but no one cares," her other self says.

The man touches her all over.
He runs his fingers through her hair.
"I love you," he whispers into her ear.
His heated breath stirs her heart.

"I can't do this," she tells herself.
"Why not? It doesn't matter either way," says her other part.
"It isn't like in the movies or on a television show," she reasons.
"Oh, but it can be. You can still get high."

It doesn't make sense.
She feels this way about herself.
The fire inside stirs until it burns even more.
"I can't stop myself."
"Good. Go and do it."
"Will it be over if I do?"
"Maybe. Maybe not. I don't know."

She reaches down,
Her hand getting closer to where she ached to be released.
“No, stop it!”
“Yes. Continue.”
“It’s wrong of me. I need to stop dreaming about him.”
Her fingers touch the waistline of her plain white underwear.

“He will notice you more if you appear sick,” her other self says.
She reaches under the cotton fabric,
Running her fingers along her aching spot.
“That’s just insane,” she claims.
“It’s romantic and will give you a high like no other.”
“No, it’s wrong. I know it’s wrong.”

Her right index finger pokes at her wetness.
Her legs tighten up with excitement.
“I really shouldn’t be doing this.”
“It doesn’t matter. You’re screwed either way.”
She rubs her finger along her wet area,
Allowing a gasp to explode from her dry lips.

She hungers for someone.
She mentally pictures someone loving her.
“That’s the spirit.”

"Why are you doing this to me?"
She begins to make faster motions.
An entire sleuth of emotions rush through her.
It feels electric.

She goes on and on,
Struggling to stifle her screams of delight.
"I'm definitely a sinner," she told herself,
Feeling on the brink of tears.
"Yeah, but no one cares."
"Don't you get it?! This is wrong!"
"What? Romanticizing mental illness is okay with me."

Finished, she lays back and breathes.
Guilt travels through her.
"I'm an idiot."
"Yeah, but you're still good to me," her brain tells her.
"I deserve to be hated."
"You deserve to be deprived."

Tears gather in her eyes,
Overflowing onto her cheeks,
Dripping from her chin onto her bright pink sweater.
"Why do I give in?"
"You're weak."

The Spice You Give

Baby boy, can you handle my demons?
Take me away.
I want to have a bite of that forbidden apple.
I want to taste your sweet honey.

The smell of your hair,
I cannot resist it.
The smell of your skin,
Drenched in sweat,
I cannot resist it.

Run your fingers through my hair.
Dip them into my sweet nectar.
I want you inside me.
I want to scream your name.

Take me to the best climax ever.
Push me beyond my limits.
Shake me to the core.
I want you.

I want to have a bite.

I want to have a taste of your sweetness.
Your heart has teeth.
My heart is bittersweet.

Wrap your arms around me.
Keep me within your warm embrace.
Let us spark one another.
We are magnets of the opposite poles.

I see you there.
Your emerald eyes look as pure as crystals.
I can see through to your soul.
Steal away my angel wings.

I am going to Hell for this sin.
Hopefully, God can forgive me.
I do not think he ever will.
This bittersweet sin,
Eyes of such sorrow crave this kind of attention.

I want your seed planted inside of me.
I want to carry a part of you.
This is what I crave.
This will be the death of everything I am meant to be.

I do not care who I have become.
It is us together.
You and I are one in the same.
We want the same thing.
Why not go for it?

Keep me warm forever.
I want to remain this way forever.
The hotness is something I crave.
I need your attention only on me.

The World

These words are how I view the world.
Well, most of these words.
Some of these words are purely fictional tales.
It’s up to you to choose.

You may not see the world the same way I do.
That’s okay with me.
Deep within my heart,
I can carry myself along this river I’ve created.

You may very well have arguments.
Come to me with them.

I'll tell you the truth.
I'll tell you the way I really feel.

What am I thinking?
What's on my mind?
Honestly, I don't even know half the time.
Please, don't question me on something like this.

The way I view the world,
What I feel,
It's all different.
I'm different.
So, please, don't come to me with your sorry butt.

I can't help the way I see the world.
It's cold and it's cruel.
Things are seriously messed up.
I'm seriously messed up.

If you can't take me as I am,
You don't need me.
Coming with your arguments.
That doesn't me cutting me to pieces.

If you want to talk,

I'll talk.
Please, talk to me.
I talk back.
In fact, I talk a lot.

Are you open?
I know I am.
I'll be honest.
I'm an honest woman.
I don't lie.
Well, I don't lie most of the time at least.

If you're willing to expose yourself,
I'm willing to expose myself.
Please, come to me.
Let's sit down and have a nice chat.

I'm tired.
I'm tired of the world.
I'm tired of everything.
That's how I really feel.

My strength needs some restoring.
Who can hold me up?
No one listens to me.

No one pays enough attention.

This Person is Me

I hate being afraid.
I shouldn't have to be afraid.
It's time for me to embrace myself.
No matter how hard it is,
No matter how annoying I am to others,
I need to be myself.

It's time for me to take a stand.
It's time for me to stop whining.
I am who I am.
It's time for me to understand that.

I'm so paranoid.
Maybe people don't think I'm annoying.
Maybe it's just me who thinks that.
It surely doesn't help when people make that statement.

One way or another,
I need to start seeing my beautiful self.
One way or another,
I need to accept the person I am.

My heart is like a lovely flower,
Blooming amidst the others.
My heart sings a song,
Just like all the others.
Listen closely to this melody.

This person is me.
This person is me.
I need to repeat this repeatedly.
This person is me.
This person is me.
I need to start believing it.

I need to be who I am.
It hurts when I cannot be who I am.
Just like the wind on my breath,
Just like the noise I make,
I exist right here and right now.

In this very moment,
I need to be powerful.
This person is me.
This person is me.
I'm not helpless.

I need myself more than anyone else.
Life is quite the rollercoaster.
It has its highs and it has its lows.
I'll bounce around in all of it.

Thoughts Occur to Me

"Maybe you want something to be wrong."
No, that's not right.
I know the truth.
Just because I'm not bleeding out into the floor,
Just because I'm not so severely underweight,
I feel like I'm not a priority.
There are people far worse off than me.
I already know this.
I'm not trying to create more problems for myself.

"Maybe you want attention."
No.
I'm not one to romanticize self-harm and eating disorders.
I'd be a fool to do such a thing.
I think I've scared enough people off as it is.

"Why did you only trust a man with such information?"

I confided in a woman.
This is something I hardly ever do.
Why?
Because I get judged, that's why.

"Do you ever watch triggering stuff on purpose?"
No, not really.
I often tend to avoid such things.
It's not easy to do.
A lot of these things are implemented into the media.
Accidentally finding one of these scenes doesn't make me a bad person.
I just must be careful.

"Don't you get bored?"
No, I get tired.
I get so very tired.
I sometimes don't even want to deal with this.

"Do you think you have a mental illness?"
Of course!
I just don't know which one.
Self-harm isn't just self-harm.
An eating disorder isn't just an eating disorder.
It all comes from somewhere.

"Do you have a reason to do this to yourself?"
Sometimes I do.
Sometimes I just self-harm.
Sometimes I just don't eat and I overdo it on the exercise.
It makes no sense to me.
When I think I've got it figured out,
I'm thrown for a loop.

"Did you pick this up from something you read?"
No, I did my research.
I knew from the start that something was wrong.
These behaviors aren't normal.
It's obvious.

"Is recovery a lifetime thing?"
Yes, it is.
I easily fall off the band wagon.
I'm overly emotional.
I allow my anxious and hurt feelings to get in the way.

"Does it interfere with your daily routine?"
Sometimes it does.
Sometimes I manage not to talk about it.
My mind tends to block it out at times.
I've become serious about what I do for a living.

“What do you think about inpatient treatment?”

I want to avoid that at all costs.

I can’t allow people to take away what is mine.

I wouldn’t survive this cruel world without my offspring.

These are some of the questions I’ve been asking myself.

I don’t know why.

I’m always stuck in my head.

I think way too much.

These are some of the things the voice tells me.

No, I’m not hearing voices.

It’s the voice in my head.

I know right from wrong.

I know black from white.

I understand the line between light and dark.

I’m smart enough to figure this out.

I can’t allow myself to be defeated by my demons.

Everyone deals with their own.

Vanishing Words

Words explode inside of my brain.

I can’t just settle down.
I can’t just settle on one word.
There are just so many words to express the way that I feel.

Why do so many words twirl around inside of my head?
It doesn’t make any sense to me.
It goes on and on and on and on.
It’s a never-ending cycle.

This never ceases to amaze me.
I can even type without looking at the screen.
I’m just typing way too fast to understand it all.
I don’t understand this phenomenon.
Maybe I’m too familiar with my keyboard keys.
I don’t know.

At the same time,
I mean the exact same time,
My words vanish from my brain.
I can’t think about what it is I want to say.
I try again and again.
It never comes to me.

Sometimes it’s in the middle of the night.
Sometimes it’s in the middle of my workday.

It doesn't matter when or how.

It just comes to me.

I know.

I just contradicted myself.

There are times when it never wants to come to me.

There are times it comes to me at the most awkward moment.

It's never the same.

The words in my brain vanish.

They never come back.

They return at some point.

It's confusing me to no end.

I can't just get a clue.

My fingers want to type a million miles a minute.

Nothing comes to my mind.

Walk Away

I turn my back to you.

I walk away from you.

I allow your harsh words to bounce off me.

I am hurt and I am the one to blame.

The blade that still serves me to this very day continues to be sharp.

The shards of my heart scatter all over the floor.
It is my fault.
I am the one to blame for this calamity.

You refuse to come to me.
You reject me with all your being.
I have made a mess of things.
I have chosen to walk away.

My heart yearns for you.
Every step I take in this life agonizes me to no end.
I do not want to do this without you.
I have no choice in the matter.

My heart aches.
I am bleeding to death over here.
It is nothing new.
I am walking away.

I am hurt and I cannot stand it.
I want to jump to my death.
I want to cut myself off from this world.
All I dream about is you.

You do not care one bit.

You have made this noticeably clear to me.
I am turning around now.
I am walking away.

I left you in the distance far behind me.
It is of no surprise that my body still screams your name.
These tears will not stop their flow.
I am hurt and I am walking away.

I enter the darkness alone.
I am always in search of the light.
I do not suppose it matters to you just how hurt I am.
You have proven to me that you do not care.

Maybe you never cared.
Maybe I never cared.
It is time to stop.
It is time to walk away.

This matter continues forth inside of me.
I am hurt so bad and I am so much the one to blame.
I am the monster of all mistakes.
The words I spoke to you were hateful.

I will never see you again.

I need to stop caring if I am still caring.
I need to walk away from you.
I need to leave you far behind me.

My memories of you bring tears to my eyes.
They cause my heart to ache until the breath is gone from my lungs.
I cannot stand this.
I have a hole inside of me.
That was the place where you once resided.

You have told me to go away.
Now I must go away.
It does not matter how much pain I am in.
Maybe I have done this to myself on purpose.

I am addicted to pain.
I have caused myself endless agony time and time again.
It is uncontrollable.
I am addicted.
I am so terribly addicted.

Call me an addict.
Call me a sinner.
I have stopped caring about it.
Go away.

Go away now.

All the mistakes I have made are coming to now.
All the cruel words I have said are coming to life now.
They are choking me to death.
I am walking away.
I am hurt and it is all my fault.
I am walking away.

Wrongful Thinking

Why do I feel like I have said something I should not have?
Why do I feel like I want to cry?
I feel as if I have lost you a little bit.
You were supposed to be my friend.

I have thought of having a forbidden affair with you.
I do not know, but maybe I am crushing on you.
I am probably also just not happy with my current affairs.
I wish for so much more.

It is possible I am crushing on someone else as well.
I feel like I am cheating.
I feel like I am doing something wrong.
It is all so incoherent to me.

This sinful heart of mine,
I want it to all go away.
I thought it romantic to have an affair,
Just like what I have witnessed on television.
I have committed a sin against God.
I have committed a sin against the one I love.

I cannot be trusted.
My mind as well as my heart,
None of which can be trusted.
I heart this message loud and clear.
It is not muffled like so many of the others have been.

I need to back off.
I need to leave well enough alone.
I need to stop dragging the men along my string.
I will shake them off.
I will shatter their hearts.

I can see myself in the mirror.
Just look at the dark woman I have become!
I am not just some sweet little girl.
I am a monster!

By doing this,
I am hurting myself.
I am hurting others.
I am not being true to anything.

I have grown up well enough to know better.
Yet, I continue.
When does it end?
Where do I draw the line?
I feel like such a slut.

I need to move on.
I need to forget about these two men.
Maybe I should not see them anymore.
Maybe I should shut them out of my life.
I do not want to hurt them.

I have taken things close to being too far.
Too far would be when I lay myself in bed with them.
I have considered a third one just to spite the man I love.
I get so angry,
Nothing else matters.
Not even the relationship matters.

My heart tugs on the hearts of others.

It is not a big deal right now.
It will be a big deal later.
I need to stop this right where it is.

I am going to end up on the wrong side of everything.
I am going to end up alone.
This love is forbidden.
I have strayed far enough.

I must go back to the man who lay down beside me.
I absolutely must return to his arms.
I absolutely must not think of anyone else but him.
It is not right to do so.
Everyone will find out at some point.

This forbidden love ends.
It may be one-sided anyway.
Unrequited love?
I have no clue.
All I know is that I am not a slut.
I am returning to the annoying man beside me.

www.ingramcontent.com/pod-product-compliance
Lightning Source LLC
LaVergne TN
LVHW080552160826
845677LV00010B/1814

* 9 7 9 8 8 4 4 0 9 1 5 3 7 *